TOPPERS

Living with Light

Nicola Baxter

W

FRANKLIN WATTS

NEW YORK • LONDON • SYDNEY

What can you see when there is no light?

We need light to see colours and shapes.

Most of our light comes from the Sun.

The Sun is a huge ball of fire
a very long way away in space.

We can see and feel heat and light
from this fire here on Earth.

The Sun is so bright that it lights up the
Earth even when there are clouds
in front of it.
Never look straight at the Sun.
It could hurt your eyes.

Try this later

Sometimes the light from the Sun seems too bright.
What can we use to stop the Sun dazzling us?

Every day the Sun moves across the sky.
In the evening, it seems to disappear.
It is hidden behind the Earth
until morning.
While the Sun is hidden, it is dark.

Try this later
Draw a picture of your school and show where
the Sun is in the middle of the day.

When the Sun is not shining,
we can use other kinds of lights.
Most of these use electricity
to make them work.

Some electric lights are very bright.

Light can shine through glass or
clear plastic.
We say that they are transparent.
We can see through them.

Try this later

How many things can you think of
that are made of glass or clear plastic?

But most things are not transparent.
Light cannot shine through them.
Where the light cannot reach, it is dark.
The dark place is called a shadow.

Try this later
Shine a bright light on to the wall.
Then put your hands in front of the light
and try to make shadow shapes.

At night there is not much light.

Some animals sleep in the daytime and come out when it is dark.

Their eyes can see better than ours can at night.

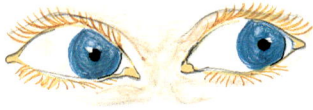

Our eyes need a lot of light to see well.
The light goes into our eyes through
the black part in the middle.
It is called the pupil.

Try this later
Look at your pupils in a mirror after
you have been in a bright light.
Then sit quietly with your hands over your eyes
for two minutes. Look in the mirror again.
Your pupils get bigger to let in more light.

Lights can help us to notice things,
especially in the dark.
They can be used just for fun...

or as signals to give a message.
They can tell other drivers which
way a car is turning.
What other light signals can
you think of?

Nothing can live without light.
Green plants can make their own food
using light from the Sun.
Insects and animals eat the plants.
People eat some of the
plants and animals.
Without light from the Sun,
there would not be anything to eat at all!

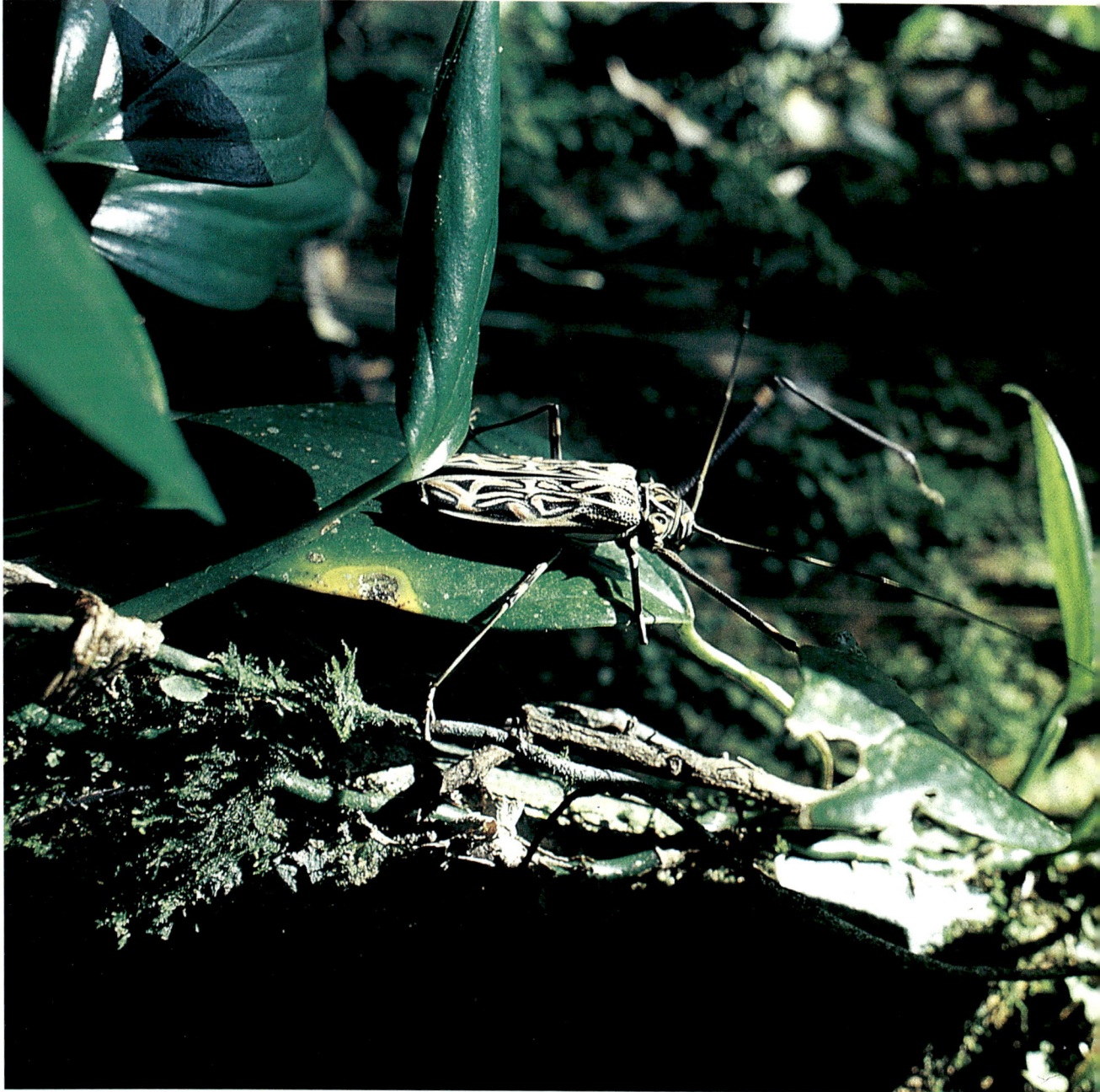

Index

© 1995 Franklin Watts
This edition 1997

Franklin Watts
96 Leonard Street
London EC2A 4RH

Franklin Watts Australia
14 Mars Road
Lane Cove, NSW 2066

Dewey Decimal Classification
Number 535
ISBN: 0 7496 1967 8

A CIP catalogue record for
this book is available from the
British Library.

Editor: Sarah Ridley

Designer: Nina Kingsbury

Illustrator: Michael Evans

The publishers would like to thank
Carol Olivier, Jason Botross and
Leanne Bates of Kenmont Primary

School for their help with
this book.

Photographs: Bruce Coleman
Ltd 17; Eye Ubiquitous 11;
Robert Harding Picture
Library 5, 9, 14, 20; Hutchison
Library 6; Peter Millard cover,
2, 3, 18; Natural History
Photographic Library 23;
Oxford Scientific Films 12.

Printed in Malaysia